Ocean Adventure

The Story of Joshua Slocum

Paul May

Contents

OXFORD UNIVERSITY PRESS

Great Clarendon Street, Oxford OX2 6DP

Oxford University Press is a department of the University of Oxford. It furthers the University's objective of excellence in research, scholarship, and education by publishing worldwide in

Oxford New York

Auckland Cape Town Dar es Salaam Hong Kong Karachi Kuala Lumpur Madrid Melbourne Mexico City Nairobi New Delhi Shanghai Taipei Toronto

With offices in
Argentina Austria Brazil Chile Czech Republic France Greece Guatemala Hungary Italy Japan Poland Portugal Singapore South Korea Switzerland Thailand Turkey Ukraine Vietnam

Oxford is a registered trade mark of Oxford University Press in the UK and in certain other countries

First published 2003

British Library Cataloguing in Publication Data

Data available

ISBN: 978-0-19-919533-6

10 9 8 7 6

True Stories Pack 1 (one of each title) ISBN 978-0-19-919537-4
True Stories Pack 1 Class Pack (six of each title) ISBN 978-0-19-919536-7

Acknowledgements

The publisher would like to thank the following for permission to reproduce photographs:

New Bedford Whaling Museum: p 6

Front cover backgound photo: Digital Vision Ltd
Inset photo: New Bedford Whaling Museum
Back cover: New Bedford Whaling Museum

Illustrations are by Janek Matysiak
Maps are by Stefan Chabluk

Printed in China by Imago

Introduction

More than 100 years ago a man called Joshua Slocum had a ship called the *Spray*.

He wanted to be the first person to sail all the way around the world on his own!

This is the story of what happened to him.

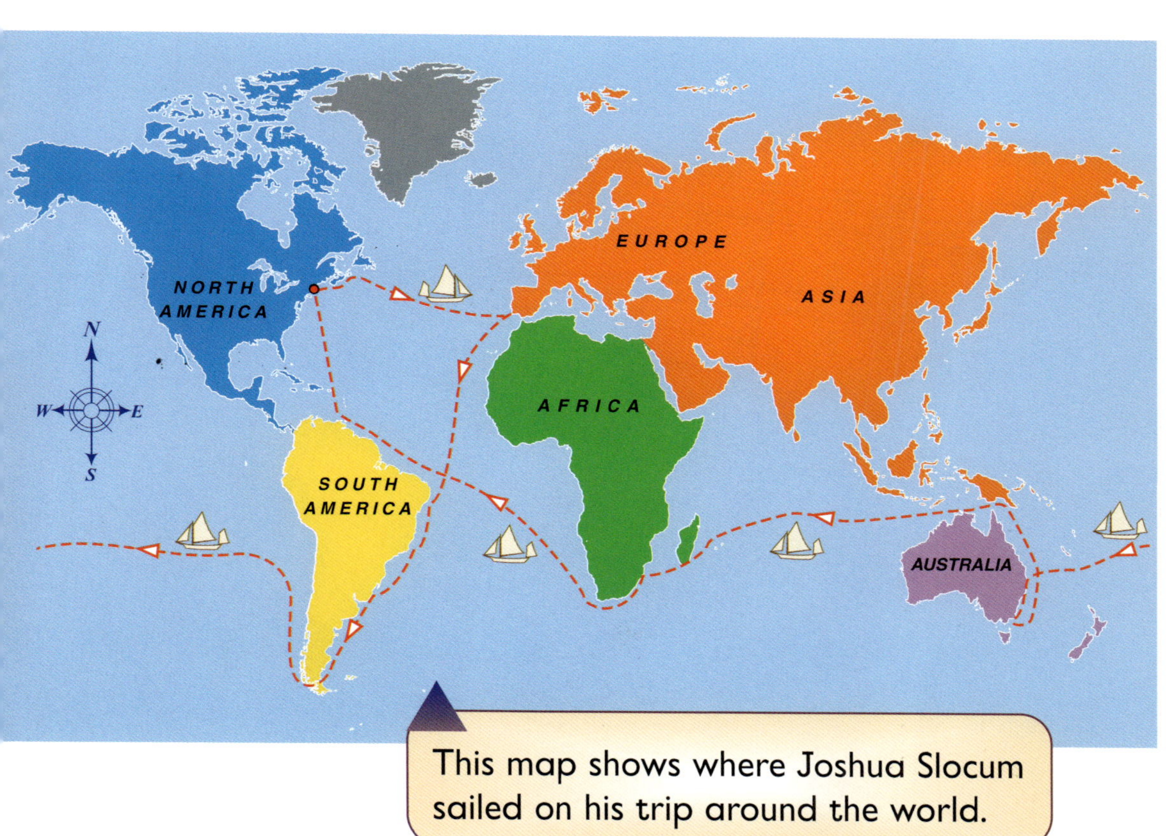

This map shows where Joshua Slocum sailed on his trip around the world.

Chapter 1

The Spray

Joshua Slocum loved sailing.

He sailed in fishing boats and steamships and tall sailing ships. But he wanted to do something different.

"I'll give you a ship," an old sailor said, "if you can fix her!"

The ship was called the *Spray*.

"She's a wreck!" said Captain Slocum. "But I'll make her like new again."

When he had finished, the *Spray* sat on the water like a swan.

"But what will you do with her?" people asked.

"I'll sail her right around the world on my own," said the Captain.

Chapter 2

Alone

On 24th April 1895 Captain Slocum sailed away from Boston, USA on the *Spray*.

The land disappeared. One by one the lights winked out.

The wide Atlantic **Ocean** stretched ahead.

Slocum's ship, the *Spray*

Captain Slocum felt lonely, but then he had an idea. He began to sing. He sang very badly, but porpoises leapt over the waves, and old turtles poked their heads up to listen.

"Now I feel better!" the Captain laughed.

Chapter 3

A Ghostly Sailor

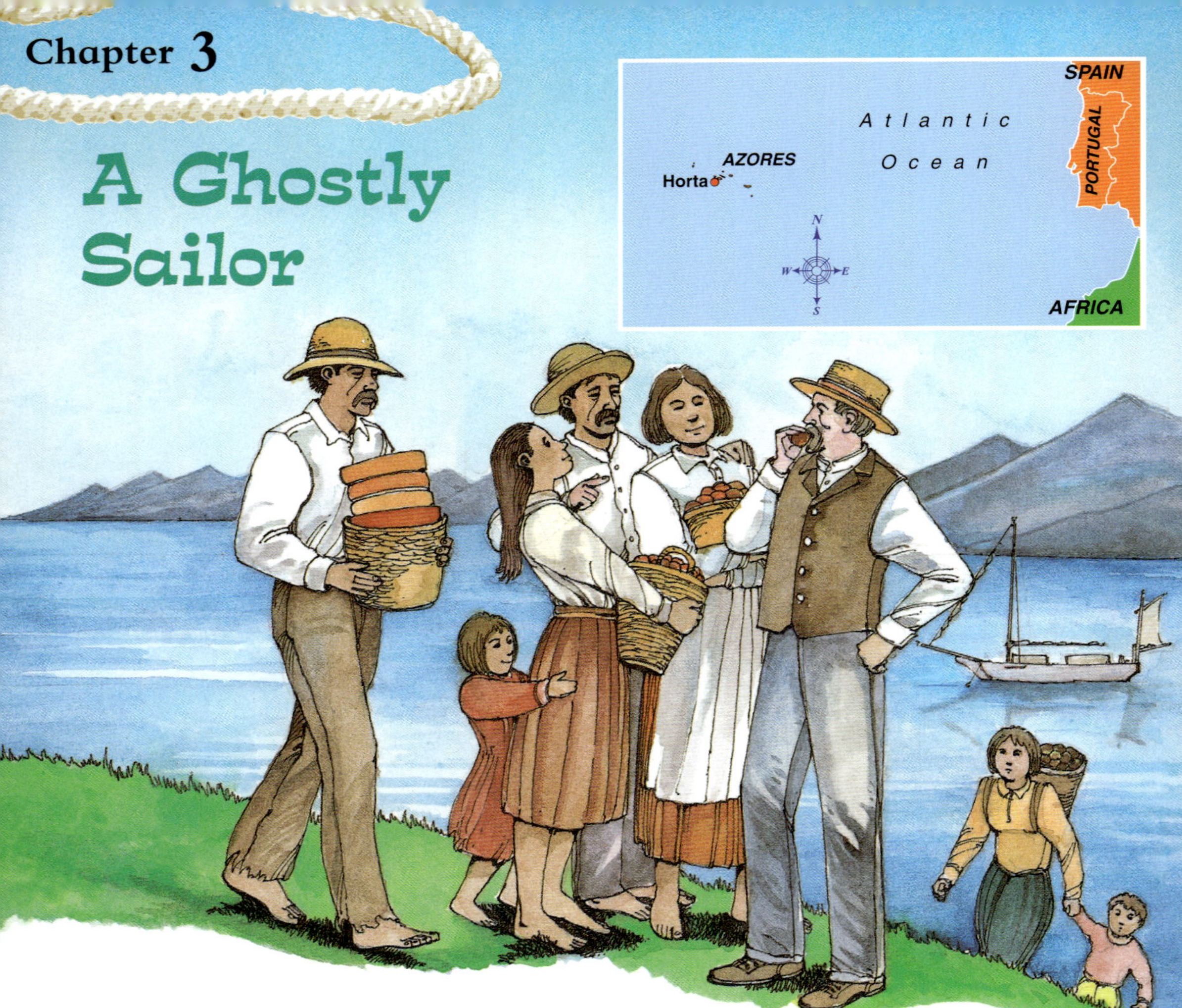

The *Spray* came to an island called Horta.

People gave Captain Slocum plums and cheese to eat. Soon his stomach began to ache.

The Captain had a fever and he lay on his bunk. He thought he saw a ghostly sailor steering the *Spray*!

For three days the Captain was ill.

For three days the ghostly sailor steered.

But when the Captain was well again, the sailor had gone.

"I must have been *very* ill," said Captain Slocum, and he threw the plums into the sea!

Chapter 4

Pirate Trouble

The *Spray* sailed into Gibraltar.

"Watch out for pirates," warned a sailor. "When you leave, keep well away from land."

Captain Slocum set sail. When he looked back, a boat full of pirates was chasing him.

The *Spray* sailed fast, but the pirates sailed faster. They were about to strike, when a huge wave crashed down on their boat, and smashed it to pieces!

The *Spray* and the Captain were safe.

Chapter 5

On the Beach

Captain Slocum sailed along the coast of Brazil, then he made a bad mistake.

He sailed onto a beach by accident. The *Spray* was stuck!

He put the **anchor** into his **dinghy** and rowed out through the crashing waves.

He stood up and threw the anchor.

The boat tipped and the Captain fell into the sea.

"Help!" he shouted. "I can't swim!"

He went under water three times. He thought he was going to die. Somehow he grabbed his boat and paddled back to shore.

"I won't make that mistake again," he gasped.

Chapter 6

Black Pedro

Captain Slocum sailed towards Cape Horn. The wind blew hard as Captain Slocum anchored in a bay.

Then the wind dropped and canoes full of pirates raced toward the *Spray*. Their leader was Black Pedro, the most terrible pirate of all.

"I must pretend I'm not alone," the Captain thought.

He dressed a piece of wood to look like another man.

But the pirates still came nearer, so the Captain fired his gun.

Black Pedro yelled, and the canoes raced back to the islands.

That night Captain Slocum sprinkled nails on the deck of the *Spray*. Then he went to sleep.

The cries of the pirates woke him. They had stepped on the nails with their bare feet! They howled as they ran away.

The *Spray* sailed on across the Pacific Ocean. The Captain looked at the moon and stars to help him find his way.

Then he did a clever thing. He made the *Spray* steer herself while he sat inside and read his books!

Chapter 7

Australia

At last the *Spray* reached Australia. People were amazed.

"The *Spray* came flying into port like a bird," the newspapers said, "and only one man could be seen on board."

The *Spray* sailed around Australia. The water was green and turquoise and blue.

COOKTOWN HERALD

The *Spray* came flying into port like a bird. It seemed strange that only one man could be seen on board working the craft.

On Thursday Island hundreds of people danced in the firelight. Some were painted like emus and kangaroos. Some were painted like frogs and skeletons.

They made music with pieces of wood and bone.

Chapter 8

A Hungry Goat

AFRICA
Atlantic Ocean
St Helena

The Captain sailed on.

"Soon I will be home," he said.

But then he made another bad mistake. In St Helena he took a goat on board for company! The goat ate the sails and ropes. It ate the Captain's straw hat and the Captain's **charts**!

Now the Captain had to *remember* his way home.

"I need my charts,' he said. "I wish I'd never seen that goat!"

At last the Captain saw a lighthouse flashing.

"Now I know where I am," he thought. "It will be easy to get home."

But he was wrong!

Chapter 9

Home at Last

Lightning crackled and thunder roared. A **hurricane** whirled around the *Spray*, but it did not harm her.

She sailed on into calm green water, and Captain Slocum saw land ahead of him.

"*Spray*, ahoy!" called a voice, and the Captain knew that he was home in Boston.

He had sailed 46,000 miles. It had taken him three years and two months, but now the voyage was over.

He had sailed alone around the world!

Glossary

anchor a piece of metal fixed to a rope or chain. It stops a ship from moving.

chart a map that sailors use to find their way

dinghy a small rowing boat

hurricane a fierce storm

ocean a very wide sea. Most of the Earth is covered by the four oceans. They are called the Atlantic Ocean, the Pacific Ocean, the Indian Ocean, and the Arctic Ocean.

Index